One

Woman's

Attempt

to

figure

out

what

is

happening.

Lori Vekre

First Printing, November 2015

Printed in The United States of America

The Library of Congress has catalogued this edition as follows:
Vekre, Lori:
One Woman's Attempt to figure out What is Happening

First Edition 5871301

One Woman's Attempt

to figure out

what is happening

in contemporary photographs

Lori Vekre

Which country knows it?[2]

Photographers: Dan Meredith and Sophia Miller

www.ingramcontent.com/pod-product-compliance
Lightning Source LLC
Chambersburg PA
CBHW050928290526
45792CB00002B/926